Dedication

*To every soul who has ever been afraid to live because your innocence died...you can be made a new creature and roam freely, as I have. **<u>Believe</u>** you can **<u>be</u> <u>alive</u>,** again.*

False God

(fahls-gaud)

n.

1) any internal or external influence which tries to convince you that you are not worthy of greatness;

2) anything that deters you from what the true Heavenly Father has already promised

Table of Contents

INTRODUCTION

Hey you! Thank you so much for trusting me to help you eliminate fear, and move on to a life of freedom and power! Congratulations on taking one step closer to the fearless you that dwells inside! I am Sir Rashad Eugene, a faith-based life coach, and speaker on a mission to help others achieve A Royal State of Mind. A state of mind that changes your way of thinking from existing as a citizen of the world, to ruling the world around you as a servant leader, and pursuer of purpose. I have a vision to bridge the gap between millennials, and the generations before. Each possess qualities the others can benefit from. However, there are common foes we must tackle first that haunt us all...like FEAR! I wrote this book from my research, studies, and of course firsthand experience. I strive to help others through my discoveries. Fear has taken control over the thoughts, and actions of mankind for far too long. It is time to face the false God, and tell the fear inside of you that it no longer has dominion over your life. By the end of this book, you will be able to articulate what fear is, the fact that is has no control over you, and how to make it work for you rather than against you. You will be able to speak to your fears, and reclaim the navigation of your thoughts, emotions, and actions. You will be empowered to begin a new endeavor, try something you've always wanted to do, and walk with more confidence, and self-control. You will even be so excited about your new life, you'll find yourself combating others who try to speak fear over you. After all, we are not designed to feel fear, we develop it over time. We create it and we have the power to eliminate it.

Let's face our fears together...

Chapter 1: To Know Fear Is To Have No Fear

At one point in my life, I'm pretty sure I was afraid of literally everything there is to be afraid of. Animals, insects, heights, small spaces, stage fright, drowning, clowns, people in general...you name it. It wasn't until I was led to stand face to face with the fears that really haunted me, when I realized...maybe I don't actually fear everything.

I developed stage fright from witnessing other kids get judged and laughed at in school whenever they had to do any type of presentation and how it affected them. I became afraid of heights and falling to the ground because I fell backwards off a swing on a playground; just as I had achieved maximum air. The many scars and bruises I acquired convinced me that being on solid ground is a safe, wise, and painless choice going forward.

I remember overcoming stage fright in the 3rd grade because the teacher directing the play, Ms. Elle, persistently pursued me to assume the role of Charlie for Charlie and the Chocolate Factory. She said she loved my energetic curiosity, goofy nature and dramatic personality. Now that I'm an adult, I think HOW RUDE! Goofy?! Dramatic?! On the contrary, she said people would love to see that on stage because it fits the character, and no one else could play it, but me. Besides her interesting choice of words for a child (no matter how true they may or may not be), she planted a positive seed in me that I had something no one else had.

I recall overcoming heights at camp in 5th grade with the support of the cool camp leader, who all the little boys believed was a real-life superhero we would hear about sooner or later. He told me that he would be right there on the ground waiting for me to zip-line all the way down from the top of the tower. He reassured me that I could do it and I'm awesome and it'll be fun and I can trust him because he's had practice on hundreds of kids. He told me how he had inspected everything himself and he wouldn't let anything happen to me.

After I screamed all the way to the ground in laughter, I remember telling him "Mr. Joseph, I can't believe I let you talk me into this but you were right! SO FUN!" We have a tendency as humans to be less afraid of something if we are formally introduced to new ideas by someone we trust. Once we mature through a bit of the fear, we grow to realize we possess the courage to do anything our hearts desire. We are powerful creatures with minds that have no limits of imagination, therefore no limits of possibilities. You are more brave and courageous than you know, especially given the right motive.

Fear derives from many factors in life. Once you can identify the root causes of your fears, you can speak to them and pluck the power you gave them from your memory. Some incidents in life which plant fear seeds are traumatic experiences (whether as a child or an adult), fear inherited from your parents' fears, and fear seeds planted by guardians, peers, and visual influences. Even things our mothers may have been afraid of when we were in the womb can affect us.

Some of the major fears that restrict us all from making the best decisions for ourselves are fear of rejection, failure, pain, being alone, being judged, losing control, missing out, and change. Whatever the fear, I believe you can overcome it with my 'Letter to Little Me' strategy. You'll learn how to do that later on in this book, but for now I want to continue grooming your mind, heart, and spirit in preparation for your breakthrough victory.

So, sometimes we have to speak aloud all the great aspects of a situation instead of giving in to fear, like I did with Ms. Elle and Mr. Joseph. The Bible says there's power in the tongue, so always speak well to live well...(*now breathe. Inhale and exhale*).

Chapter 2: Render Fear Powerless

If you have ever heard me speak, you might have picked up that I am a life coach, and speaker who operates from a spiritual place. I have often said, if you are not a believer, at least consider the Bible to be the oldest book in the world about the Creator, and His son, the most famous man to walk the Earth. According to the Bible, 1 Samuel 12:24 says "Only fear the LORD, and serve Him in truth with all your heart." This statement beginning with "only" tells us that even back then, there was nothing to fear but God.

Any other time fear is mentioned in the Bible when not referencing God or when God is speaking it says "fear not" and "be not afraid." These are ideas we should continue to live by today. We should "only" fear the Creator, the higher power, and not the earthly things we obliviously relinquish power to.

We were not created to be fearful. So, because we create fear for ourselves, we can dethrone its power and influence. What's funny is, to be God-fearing or to fear God in the Bible days was not used in the same context that fear is used in modern times; being afraid of someone or something. To fear God is to understand His word, respect His word, and apply His word to your life. It's to live by His word, and give up the very things that separate us from Him. To fear God is to be afraid of His absence from you. To achieve God's love is to be without man-made fears. Only then will you feel in control and powerful.

Whatever has control over our thoughts, and actions has the power. We give power to people when we fear their ridicule. We give power to failure when we let thoughts of rejection, inadequacy and other negative theories take over. We give power to giants in our lives when we belittle ourselves out of fear of not being enough. We give control over our thoughts, and actions to ideas that have not actually come to fruition but only live in our imaginations.

All the negative thoughts you have ever had about ANYTHING that has ever held you back in life are LIES. Stop allowing people to tell you what you can't do because they don't believe they can. Stop allowing people to tell you that you can't succeed in life because they never have. Hurting people, hurt people. Don't blame them for their ignorance, but educate them. If you are not at a place where you feel comfort, and confidence in doing that, then pray for them. Avoid them until you are strong enough to say "No, maybe you aren't sure of yourself but I know what I am capable of, and until you can say the same, I would appreciate you keeping your concerns private...but thank you for caring!"

So, when you can identify and cast out the causes of fear in your life, you drain it of its power, and it has to wither, and die. You are not fearful because you lack strength, you are fearful because you don't know how to use your strength...(*now breathe. Inhale and exhale*).

Chapter 3: Fight Fear With Focus

Some say the opposite of fear is courage. I beg to differ. They are more coheres than opposites to me. Courage is the ability to do something that frightens you. That means you are afraid but you do it anyway; they work, and exist together. For me, the opposite of fear is focus because it ignores fear. Both fear, and focus are motives; opposing motives. Fear causes you to run at the first sign of danger, retreat from attention, and refuse trying things you don't understand, or don't think you can do. Focus causes you to work towards survival in the face of danger, command attention to accomplish something good, and do whatever is necessary to achieve goals. Fear is a bad habit of negative thought processing created from imagination, whereas focus is a good, self-disciplined obsession of positive thought processing to achieve a goal.

Without focus you will fall prey to fear and only tap into courage when you build up enough of it to get you through an immediate circumstance. I don't offer attention to fears. I just tell myself to obsess over an area I want to focus on, and let fear disappear on its own. It goes away without me even thinking about it. Focus also involves courage, which helps build confidence.

With focus and confidence you can do things you were once afraid to do because you no longer have concern of the what if's, and might be's. You then only think of the awesome possibilities, rewards, and fruits of your labor. The goal is not to build courage in the midst of your fears. The goal is to find a focus, and build your love, and obsession over the outcomes, and dreams you want to achieve. The goal is to be so focused that fear is not a deciding factor in your thoughts, and actions. Fear will disappear, and you'll only focus on the finish.

So, if you have no focal point, you have no motive to fight through every obstacle you'll face. Find a focus to replace fear, and you'll find a new outlook on life...(*now breathe. Inhale and exhale*).

Chapter 4: Don't Confuse Fear With Caution

As described by many great speakers, fear is False Evidence Appearing Real. In the dictionary, you will find fear to be "an unpleasant emotion caused by the belief that someone or something is dangerous, likely to cause pain, or a threat." The fact that 'belief' is mentioned in the definition, helps me to understand fear is a made-up story we force ourselves to think is true. Fear is being afraid of something that hasn't even happened, and probably never will. Fear makes us sound crazy!

Caution, on the other hand, is understandable, as it means "care taken to avoid danger or mistakes." I can always understand someone who says "I cannot walk that way because there is a 'caution sign' or I have information that tells me it is not a favorable road." However, I cannot digest someone saying "I can't walk that way because I'm afraid of what's down that road or I don't know what is down that road." When we come to an unknown road, or opportunity in life, we must ask ourselves a few questions:

1. What do I know about this road that should warrant caution?

2. Do I sense danger that actually exists or imaginary fear?

3. What is the best/worst that could happen?

4. Do I take another road or will turning away now be the end of my journey?

(**1. What do I know about this road that should warrant caution?**)

If fear is an unpleasant emotion caused by the belief that danger exists, we have to challenge that, and determine where this 'belief' is stemming from. There was a bad seed planted somewhere along the way, that caused us to believe danger lurks around unknown, or unseen corners. In addition, mankind has taught us to fear that which we do not understand, identify with, or recognize. This means we create a fear seed in our minds, adopted from other peoples' thoughts. Plus, outside influences deepen our fear by capitalizing on what we've already accepted as danger on our own.

This becomes a system of fertilizing the self-planted-fear-seed, while others plant more fear seeds, and we end up watering them all. We allow them to grow and grant them authority over our thoughts, emotions, and actions. Fear becomes a deep root that prevents motion in a positive direction. We have given power to unpleasant emotions caused by the belief that danger exists...even though NOTHING has happened to prove there is danger. Most of the time there is no warrant of real caution; only man-made fear.

(**2. Do I sense danger that actually exists or imaginary fear?**)

Fear is not always born from experience, as caution is. When we take heed to caution, it is because someone, or something has WARNED us that hurt, harm, or danger CAN SURELY lie ahead. When we retreat, and give power to fear, it is because someone, or something has CONVINCED us that hurt, harm, or danger MIGHT lie ahead. Terms such as 'warning,' and 'can surely' will always be supported by facts in any situation. Words such as 'convince,' and 'might' are manipulative words of suggestion, attempt to control, and open-ended discoveries.

When we proceed with caution, it's usually because we know the good, and bad of a situation. We at least have an idea for what we're up against, and therefore can make an informed decision on what would be best. When we sit on our thoughts, and actions regarding untested ideas because of fear, we are depriving ourselves of new possibilities, and opportunities to pioneer something great. When it comes to taking chances in life, phrases like 'better safe than sorry' are a cop-out. I say, if you want to advance, take a chance!

(3. What is the best/worst that could happen?)

With any decision we make in life, there are two general outcomes: good, or bad. The believer understands that ALL things work together for our good, but for the sake of the argument, let's entertain this concept.

Ok, drive with me. You're stuck in traffic, and it's 30 minutes before you have to be at work. You're usually only a few minutes late, and your boss doesn't flip out on you about punctuality. Thank God! However, you left earlier than usual this morning. You're approaching a side street that you have often wondered could be a short cut, but you have been too afraid to try it, fearing you might actually arrive to work even later...stay with me.

Considering you left earlier than usual, you take a chance, and turn on the side street. You cut a lot of traffic, and arrive to work 15 minutes early! That was a good outcome for the decision you made! A decision you were once fearful to try. The side street has now become a part of your routine route. A week later, your boss is elated that you have "put forth an effort to arrive on time, and support your team better," in their eyes.

The worst that could've happened is, you made a bad decision to turn down a side street that made you later than usual, and your boss would have a serious conversation with you, or a form for you to sign. Either way it would've ended, you took a chance, and now have the experience to warn, or inform someone else of your discovery.

The lesson in this is not that finding short cuts in life is good. The lesson is, you can either do what is common, and stay on the road in traffic with other people who continue to do the same thing every day, and get the same results, OR you can do something extraordinary, and take the road less traveled; yielding a change in your confidence because you had the courage to take a chance that paid off.

(4. Do I take another road or will turning away now be the end of my journey?)

I've learned to never become detached from my dreams because of fear. We should never turn away from our destiny because we don't understand everything along the way. We should never abandon our dreams to pick up, and carry fear. It's a dead weight that prevents us from moving forward.

In the late 1800s, Henry Ford worked with electricity, and engineering, and became fascinated with building automobiles, which were all fairly new concepts back then. With the help of a couple friends, he built his first automobile called the Ford Quadricycle, but was unhappy with its power and functionalities. He continued to work with company after company, seeking to perfect his vision of a powerful vehicle he could sale at a lower price than the competitors.

Soon after, he decided to hire a team of people who could do all the things he couldn't do to create his vision. He led this team as a servant leader, and founded his own Ford Motor Company, which is still an award-winning vehicle brand today! He wasn't deterred from his dream because of what he couldn't do. Instead, he hired people who could fill in those missing elements. He just decided to take a different avenue to achieve what he wanted to do as a service to America. Mission accomplished? Exactly.

Henry Ford was so focused that turning around was not an option for him. He didn't have fear that his ideas wouldn't work. He only had fear that he would not find the answers. Fear of failure should not turn you away from what you want. Once you identify the end result you hope to achieve, develop a full proof plan of approach to focus on. When you are focused, you are determined, and will stop at nothing to achieve your goal. Find something to focus on and obsess over it.

So, remember to take caution into consideration, but don't let it fester into fear, and keep you from all the accomplishments life has in store for you...(*now breathe. Inhale and exhale*).

Chapter 5: Fear As A Weapon

It's an incredible feeling when you can want something so much, you only fear losing it. Fear of lose is a healthy fear because it births desire and desire births drive and drive births focus. Have you ever heard crazy stories of parents, especially mothers, defending their children from animals, or other kids? They are so afraid of something happening to their children that they become focused on protecting them. Fear of animals, or police, or being hurt in any way dissipates, and there is only survival, and fight left on their minds.

It is in those moments, when we feel like our backs are against the wall, that we come out swinging. When we feel like it's all, or nothing. Fight because we have no outlet for flight. It is then, that we discover just how strong, clever, and quick we are. We unveil what we are truly capable of. It is when we fear the end, that we tap into our power to change it.

Fear only controls us in whatever way we allow it to. I feared I would be bored in high school, and drop out because the work was too easy (backwards and crazy, right? I know). So, I made it fun by joining theatre, and I put together the school's first dance team. I feared being broke when I first started working, so I constantly worked overtime just to have a savings cushion. I feared for the youth, and young adults of the world, so I started to make a difference at my church. I became a leader, and helped pioneer new ideas.

Fear can consume you, or it can fuel you. It's how we process fear that determines how it affects us. Like anger, fear can birth creativity. What I feared was remedied by the ideas I put into motion to avoid the outcomes I didn't want to experience. Whatever you fear can be overcome depending on how you digest the situation. You just have to decide that you want a better outcome, and the ideas will flow to you to get you through.

Fear of failure can change your outlook on life. Something I've learned is, if you ever hit rock bottom, you get a better view of the top. When I lost my last job, that felt like the bottom for me, but I knew I would be alright. When I later ran out of unemployment funds and began collecting food stamps and my truck began to break down and my health was failing me, then I found rock bottom.

I found myself looking over my life, everything good, everything bad, and it forced me to look to the new life I want for myself. I looked up, and saw just how far the top is, but I also saw what brought me to the bottom. I saw all the mistakes I made that prevented me from reaching the top. Through prayer and supplication, I began to have visions of my future. That's what visions are. Visions are postcards from the future, only they don't say "wish you were here." Instead, they say, "I can't wait for you to get here!"

I am afraid I won't fulfill everything God has in store for me to do. I am afraid I will make a mistake, and miss something that will separate me from the visions He's given me. So, I do a little more each day to be of service as He wants me to be. I work hard to secure my future. I use fear to fuel me on this ride to the top that I know I can reach because I've seen it, and I believe it.

So, turn your fear into fuel (for your focus). Don't be afraid of the fall. As the living legend Les Brown said, "If you fall down, make sure you fall on your back because if you can look up, you can get up!"...(*now breathe. Inhale and exhale*).

Chapter 6: Fear Makes You Feeble

Often times when playing sports, and different activities in school, or in the neighborhood as a kid, I was chosen last for a long while. It made me feel as if no one liked me or I wasn't good enough or no one wanted to play with me. In all fairness, I didn't want to actually play all the time. I just wanted to feel included, and involved in something. It wasn't until I got comfortable in a game, understood how it worked, and discovered new strengths in my positions, that I got as good as the other kids, and in time, a force to be reckoned with. Eventually, I became a first round pick, and sometimes Team Captain.

When I examine this as an adult, I think about the fact that I am very transparent, a true Virgo, and no matter the circumstance I express my emotions with my face. I was scared and confused back then when it came to new games, or sports I had never played. Then it dawned on me...no one wanted to pick me because I looked afraid! No one felt confident that I could potentially help them win because I looked too afraid to even participate. My face basically told them, "Do not pick me! I will make you lose because I don't know what I'm doing!"

No matter how much you may, or may not know someone, we all share a common gift that tells us certain things about each other. It's called discernment.

We can almost smell fear on other humans. We can sense a certain level of confidence, charisma, anger, joy, and so many other emotions, and states of mind. In these moments, we will either mirror each other as a form of comfort, or reject each other in some capacity. In my case, I was rejected by being ignored, overlooked, and whispered about. Normally, I wouldn't care to elaborate about whispers, and being ignored, but in this sense they deserve some attention.

When I was waiting to be picked for sports, and activities, I appeared to be fearful. Because I appeared to be fearful, I was rejected by being ignored, and whispered about. Being fearful made me look weak, unfit, and inadequate. Kids are not generally concerned with including everyone to make everyone comfortable. They want to have fun, and win! In the game of life, you don't advance because you are scared to play, and want your hand held. You advance because you are confident, enthusiastic, and you play to win!

Depending on the situation, playing to win sounds easier said than done. Fear has an innate ability to break down your confidence, enthusiasm, focus, courage, drive, and positive energy. Without those things, you're susceptible to low self-esteem, laziness, procrastination, depression, and even bitterness. Fear is a dark cloud, and when you're already in a dark place, it can consume you.

In life, you have to build a strong foundation of

love, and understanding for who you are, and what you are capable of. You have to love yourself enough to want, seek, and pursue greatness. The Bible says we are more than conquerors! That means any obstacle which stands in our way, is already overcome. We just have to have faith that we will triumph (as it is promised,) and go thru the motions required to knock it down. After all, I believe we all know by now, faith without works is dead.

When I began working as a visual stylist for the first time, there was a person on my team who was never happy for me whenever I received great feedback for my work. They would throw shade, and even try to sabotage my projects in one way or another. Their daily attempts to break me became a burden, and effective on some level. I began to doubt my own abilities, lose confidence, and questioned if I was a likable person to work with (considering I was so disliked each day).

I stopped being myself in hopes I could avoid conflict. I didn't want to ask to be a part of anything outside of my own projects, so I wouldn't have to interact with that person. I diminished myself to try and please people around me. More importantly, which was probably the only positive, I humbled myself enough to not curse anyone out, or do anything the old me would've done to get even.

By this point in my life, I had developed a strong relationship with God. Because I knew Him, I had peace that surpasses all understanding. I had such joy with other areas of my life, that even though I wasn't myself for those few hours a day, I knew I would have the rest of the day, and my days off to be carefree. Fear made me feel as if it was better to fade into the background.

However, the more I worked alone, the more I realized everything I touched was completely on me. Only I would be held responsible. I had to make sure that even if I wasn't my whole self, and didn't interact much with people to prevent incidents with a team member, I needed to put my all into my work every time, every day.

My work had to be my best. I had to show the light inside of me that I knew was still there. Months later, I was promoted from being part-time because that lovely person was escorted from the building, leaving behind their full-time position to me...the Bible also says God will make your enemies your footstool.

So, fear can cripple you, but it should never knock you down. Don't ever allow others to dictate your thoughts, actions, or demeanor. Find and fall in love with yourself, and you find unbreakable strength...(*now breathe. Inhale and exhale*).

Chapter 7: Letter To Little Me

HERE WE ARE! You've made it through quite a journey! Oh! Not referring to my book. Well, I pray it resonated with you on some level, at some point, but I meant your life! You are an incredibly strong individual to have made it thus far, and for good reason. The Bible says He gives His strongest tests to His strongest warriors!

I would like to share just a few more glimpses into my journey in hopes it will help you. I find that speaking to yourself in front of a mirror is a deeply intimate experience. Depending on the "conversation," it can be fun, funny, scary, serious, or just plain weird! It is also very therapeutic. Much like writing to yourself.

There's something about getting your hurtful thoughts out into the atmosphere that helps you heal. I wrote a letter to myself, and read it out loud standing in front of a mirror. It really helped me release myself from the bondage of my fears, that derived from the most traumatic experiences in my life. Fear can develop as a result of things that have not been resolved, and need to be forgiven. Things you need to forgive yourself for, and release other people by forgiving them.

To express this, I wrote a letter to 'Little Me.' The child version of me that was traumatized, the teenager that was teased, and the young adult that had to fight. In preparation for this self-intervention, I collected 3 pictures of myself, and taped them along the edges of the mirror. One of me as a little boy, one as a teenager, and one as a young adult to represent each major phase of my life.

It was important for me to have those 3 pictures visible, so that I could feel as if I was confronting all of my past at once. It made it easier for me to speak directly to all those young men that were still hurting inside.

One thing I have learned from studying psychology is, symbolism is a perspective that takes you deeper into a thought, emotion, or circumstance. It can reveal seeds that need to be uprooted. In my case, it took me back to my past. Looking into the eyes of my young, innocent, troubled selves.

These photos, in accordance with my letter, really helped me release feelings I didn't realize I had still been harboring. This letter helped me forgive myself, and my offenders for everything that happened to me. It helped me understand that it was all for my good. I am stronger, wiser, more aware, cautious, but courageous, and excited to move on with my life!

If you can find the strength to do the same, even if you invite someone to be there because you can't do it alone, I GUARANTEE your life will be different. I'm sharing this with you solely for your breakthrough. My testimony is my pride. My testimony is important to me because of my tests results...I PASSED EACH AND EVERY

ONE OF THEM WITH FLYING COLORS BECAUSE I'M...STILL...HERE!!!

And so I wrote...

Hey Little Shad!

First, I want to say I love you and I miss you! I miss your innocence. I always keep a part of you with me to remind me that a pure heart and pure mind is achievable because it once existed in you, before the world tried to break you. I want to prepare you for your future in hopes you will fight through it as I already have. You are going to experience some ugly things from people close to you and people you don't quite know but it's ok. I'm writing so you have proof that you made it thru it all. You're going to be bullied, ridiculed, mistreated and gossiped about just because you're different. As a child, you're going to be teased for your hair, your walk, your talk, your laugh, your big smile, for wearing glasses and just for being who you are. You'll be teased for your high energy but never lose it because you love and embrace it now. You learn to accept it as who you are. As a teenager, you're going to be beaten up by cruel kids who fear you because they don't understand you. There are some who will torment you for years but if you just stick to the things that make you happy, it'll pass over. Please don't attempt to take your life because you were

29

never successful with that. All you will do is have to explain how you hurt yourself or why you are so sick and you'll waste time and energy trying to end an amazing life that hasn't yet begun. You will still be here for years to come so don't waste your time trying to die. Focus on why you are here instead. You have so many beautiful things to live for and you will get to them if you keep fighting. You're going to invite a friend into your room that you thought you could trust who's going to take advantage of you and steal your innocence. I'm so sorry for letting him in. You're going to hold on to that for a very long time but I know now that you could've at least trusted Clarissa. She was a real friend and she could have helped you release that pain years ago. Maybe if you told her, you would've had a different outlook and avoided the second time. You trusted someone again that you hardly knew as a young adult and he not only took advantage of you, he choked you and you never deserved that. It was not your fault, it absolutely was not but maybe if you resolved the first hurt you would have looked for love in a different type of person. I'm sorry I didn't catch that. You're going to be misunderstood by family and friends. Strangers will even make you second guess yourself but they are all liars! Some people you look up to will look down on you. Understand you are not beneath them, you are beside them but they looked down because that's where you held your head. I have worked very hard to protect the part of you that never died in me. As I close this letter, I feel that part growing, blooming and beaming with triumph and rebirth.

You are everything God says you are! Get to know Jesus as soon as you feel inclined and TRUST HIM with every fiber of your being! He is SO good! Once again, I apologize for my mishaps. I want you to know I forgive myself and I forgive those who have hurt us. I pray God has mercy on them. I love you deeply. Be strong. Be smart. Be spiritual. Be of service. Love God and everyone. Fight little guy.

With all the love I own,

Sir Rashad Eugene <3...(now I breathe...inhale.........and exhale).

Acknowledgments

Thank you for reading through my entire book! It's the first of many to come. It was incredibly difficult to share so much of myself to, potentially, the entire world, but I did it!

I would first like to thank God for everything He's done, everything He's doing, and everything that's to come. For whispering the details of my purpose in my ear, and allowing me to begin to bring them to fruition. For allowing me to understand every facet of my life, and use it all to service others.

I thank you my gorgeous, magnificent mother, Freddie, and my amazing brother, John, for their support beyond measure since I began my new journey in life. Thank you for the words of wisdom, and the encouragement. Thank you both for catching me when I fell, and for carrying me until I could crawl, stand, walk, run, and fly on my own. Thank you for believing in me, and for correcting me when I needed it. Thank you for noticing the seeds God planted in me, and watering them everyday.

Thank you to my stunning sisters, Helen, Tonia, and Tawanna, and my mother for showing me that a mind is truly a terrible thing to waste. You four ladies were in school, all at the same time, paving the way for us all in this family to continue to achieve greatness, and never, ever stop. Thank you all for teaching me grace, class, style, and how to have a giving heart.

Thank you Tonia for being one of my first clients, and for helping me, inadvertently, unlock parts of myself I had tucked away that needed to be set free.

To my brothers, LeAndrew and Rashed, who stand with the Lord. I thank you for the memories I have to carry with me for life. I can still hear your warm, heavy voices encouraging me to be great. I know you guys are helping guide, protect, and groom me for what's to come. Thank you my angels.

To my incomparable nieces, and nephews, Brianna, Dupreea, Charnee, Michael, John, Charnece, Javonnie, Collin, Chance, Daniyah, and Lorice. I thank you all for being such bright beacons of the future, and keeping me going with your energy, and ambitions. Next to God, and my mother, you are the reasons I work so hard to be successful. I have to be an example because you look up to me. Thank you for your admiration, and inspiration.

Thank you to my loving aunt Gloria, and my awesome brother (in law) Collin, for speaking greatness over my life before anyone else saw it...including me.

To my mentors Stephanie, Ashley, Nancy, Shalondria, and Christian. You all are my 5 Horsemen! My five point star as a guiding light in my dark skies. Thank you for your spiritual guidance, support, insight, encouragement, ideas, laughs, and friendship. Thank you all for speaking greatness into my life, and helping me blossom one petal at a time.

Thank you to the incredible Lisa Nichols (no, I do not know her...at all). But she was the first speaker I studied and followed. One thing she said which has stuck with me throughout my journey is "If you're afraid to dive, dive afraid." I took a leap into a new level of comfort called walking in my truth and I feel so liberated, powerful, and in control.

Thank you to everyone who has been for me, and against me. Thank you for your love, and your disdain. Thank you for the joy, and the pain. I needed everything I've been through to be the man I am today, and I absolutely love being *Sir Rashad Eugene!*

Love ya's!

Made in the USA
Columbia, SC
14 November 2020